Crewe House

The Royal Embassy
of
The Kingdom of Saudi Arabia

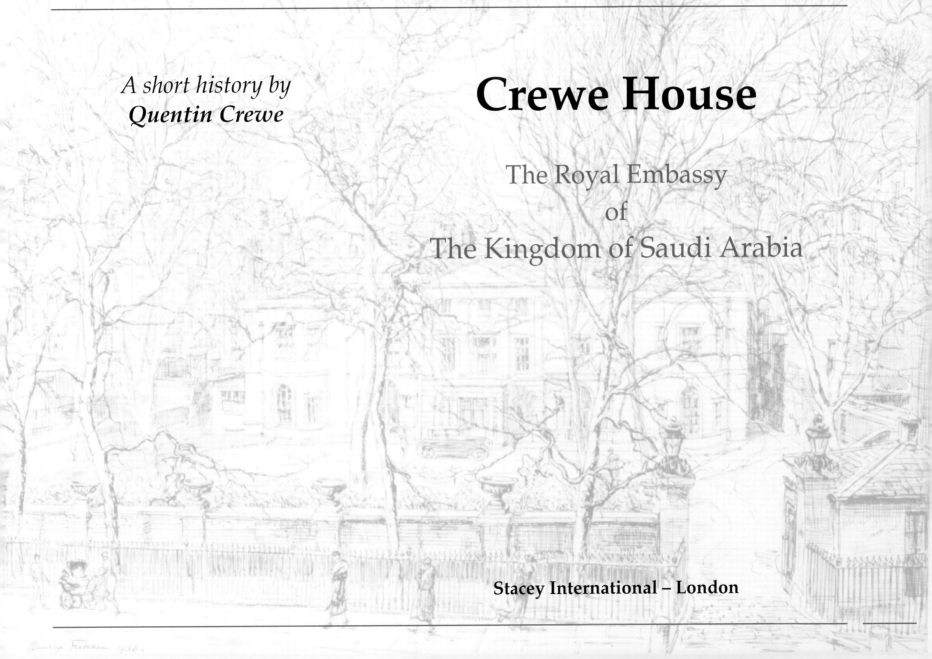

A short history by
Quentin Crewe

Crewe House

The Royal Embassy
of
The Kingdom of Saudi Arabia

Stacey International – London

Crewe House,
The Royal Embassy of
The Kingdom of Saudi Arabia
by Quentin Crewe

Published by Stacey International,
128 Kensington Church Street, London W8 4BH.
Fax: 0171 792 9288

Editor : Frances Montgomery
Art Director : Jo Cotter
© Stacey International, 1995

British Library Cataloguing-in-Publication Data
A catalogue record for this book is available from
the British Library.

ISBN 0 905743 784

Set by SX Composing Limited, Rayleigh, Essex, England
Printing and binding by Tien Wah Press, Singapore

Half-title page:	Horwood's Map of Mayfair, 1797 (1813 ed.)	
	(Guildhall Library)	
Title page:	Crewe House by Hanslip Fletcher, 1936	
	(Private Collection)	

The author thanks the following individuals who helped with the
research and preparation of this book:

Mary, Duchess of Roxburghe (daughter of the late Lord Crewe)
Victor Belcher who helped with Edward Shepherd
John Knight of Michael Lyell Associates, architect for the
    restoration of Crewe House
Felix Barker who gave wise counsel
Liz Mostyn-Owen who began the research
John Martin Robinson who completed the research with the care and
    diligence of a true scholar
The London Division of English Heritage
Richard Charlesworth of Tilcon Ltd.
Miss Ruth Harman of Sheffield City Archives
Mrs Dolores Karney who typed the manuscript

Illustrations reproduced by kind permission of the following:

Guildhall Library
British Library
Soane Museum
The Royal Commission on the Historical Monuments of England
National Portrait Gallery
Greater London Record Office

Contents

For Charity Crewe

Foreword

The discovery that Crewe House was for sale was a matter of good fortune for Saudi Arabia. The London embassy's previous quarters in Belgrave Square, although well situated, were cramped and inadequate. Crewe House was a magnificent building in itself. Until the 1930s it had been one of the best – and perhaps the most splendid – of the family stately homes in Mayfair. But when it was sold in 1933 to Thomas Tilling Ltd. additional adjacent buildings at the side and back of old Crewe House were added and converted into apartments and office space. This was vital to the needs of our embassy.

Thomas Tilling made only minor alterations to the façade on Curzon Street. Members of the Mayfair Residents' Association were apprehensive that we might make radical new changes – perhaps of a radically oriented character. This was never our intention. Proud to be the owners of one of London's great historic buildings, we were determined that any changes in the course of adapting and refurbishing the building would not only be in complete harmony with its surroundings but that the façade and forecourt of old Crewe House should be restored to their former glory.

Our second piece of good fortune was in finding Mr Quentin Crewe to provide this short history of our new embassy. He is not only a writer of panache and distinction but as a member of the last family to own the house – the family which gave it its name – he began the writing with a considerable previous knowledge of its many famous historical and political associations. The result has been just what was needed.

I take great pleasure in introducing this book to our Arab and British friends, hoping they will derive from it as much pleasure as I did.

Ghazi Algosaibi
Ambassador

Illustrations

Listed in sections in date order

* denotes that the picture is reproduced in colour

Abbrevations

G.L.R.O. – Greater London Record Office

N.M.R. – The Royal Commission on the Historical
               Monuments of England

N.P.G. – National Portrait Gallery, London

Beresford Chancellor – *Private Palaces of London*, London, 1908

Chapter One

The Building of the House

It is hard to imagine that, not much more than 250 years ago, the lane that was to become Curzon Street ran through virtually open country towards Hyde Park, which had hardly changed since the days when it was a private hunting ground of Henry VIII.

To the north, one part of Miss Davies' farm (the foundation of the Grosvenor estates and the Dukes of Westminster's fortunes) had already begun to be developed to form Grosvenor Square. A little to the east of where Crewe House now stands, the river Tyburn was still an uncovered stream, trickling from the site of the famous gallows and on into the Thames. (Fig. 1)

Regularly every year since the reign of Charles II, when it was transferred from the Haymarket, a popular fair had been held on the land to the south towards Green Park. It was known as the May Fair and eventually the whole district took its name from this event. As early as 1708, there was some opposition to the fair and gradually it became so rowdy and disreputable that it was finally banned in the mid-eighteenth century.

The fundamental changes to the area began in 1715, when Sir Nathaniel Curzon, 4th Bt (1675-1758) of Kedleston in Derbyshire bought a three-acre field bordered by the lane. One of his first acts was to build a chapel, known as the Mayfair or Curzon chapel, on the site now occupied by Sunderland House opposite Crewe House.

The first incumbent, the Reverend Alexander Keith, soon acquired a certain notoriety, for he regularly performed marriages, "without the formalities of banns or licenses", that is to say quite without any legal validity whatever.

In 1742, the authorities attempted to put a stop to Keith's activities and the chapel was closed, but this bogus man of the cloth was not easily discouraged. He moved to the other side of the street and continued his

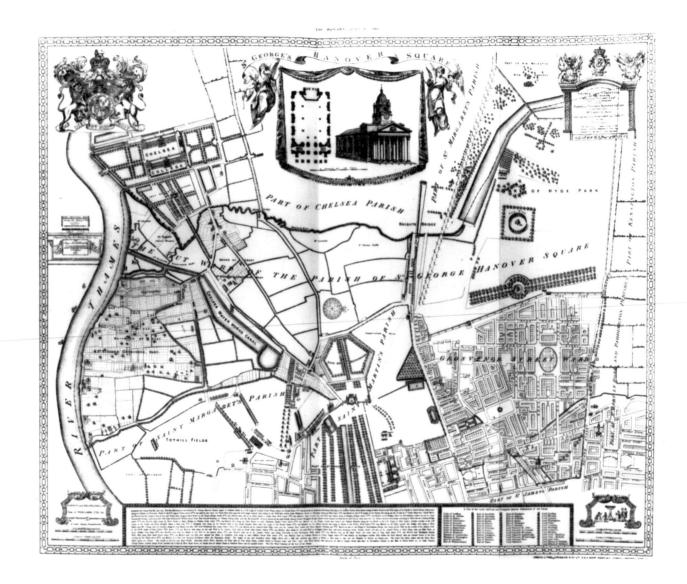

convenient services in an unauthorised chapel next to Crewe House. He put an advertisement in the *Daily Post* on 10 July 1744 announcing that "the little new chapel in Mayfair . . . is in the corner house, opposite the great chapel and within ten yards of it." Here, for one guinea, Keith was prepared, "at any hour till 4 in the afternoon" (an odd sop to legality) to perform speedy informal marriages. Among them, the Duke of Hamilton married Miss Gunning "with the ring of the bed curtain", according to Horace Walpole. In all, some 7000 unfortunate girls were said to have been deceived into spurious marriages by Keith and his assistants.

The British aristocracy having, by nature, no deep-seated disapproval of immorality, such scandals did no harm to the district. In 1730, Sir Nathaniel started to sell plots of land to builders for development and it was to prove a very profitable business, for the fashionable centre of London was to continue its westward movement for another century or more.

At this point there appeared an enterprising and unusual character, Edward Shepherd. He was by profession a plasterer, though he belonged to that small group of builder-architects in the early Georgian period who were firmly grounded in craft traditions, yet carried the ideals of the architectural text books into the realm of speculative building and managed to exercise a fair degree of competence and expertise.

We first hear of Shepherd in 1718 as the building lessee of a plot in Pollen Street and he remained a speculative builder throughout his career, although he was more than once referred to as a "famous architect" and he confidently signed the memorial to Henry Grey, Duke of Kent at Flitton in Bedfordshire "Edw:d Shepherd Arch:t".

It was perhaps his work for various grandees that gave him a more elevated status than one might have expected. In 1723-5 he was in the service of James Brydges, 1st Duke of Chandos, who employed him to

(Fig. 1) John Mackay's Map of the Parish of St George, 1725. The westward expansion of London was controlled by large, private estates. These were gradually divided up and sold to developers.

supervise the completion of his mansion at Cannons. Soon afterwards, he built two houses on the north side of Cavendish Square for the Duke and looked after building operations for him at Bridgewater and Bath, though he does not often seem to have been responsible for the actual designs of work done by local master-builders.

In 1730, when together with Gibbs and Flitcroft, he was one of the candidates for rebuilding the church of St Giles-in-the-Fields, the *Daily Post* described him as "that ingenious architect Edward Shepherd Esq., who built the Duke of Kent's fine house in St James's Square, the Earls of Thanet's and Albemarle's in Grosvenor Square, and many other magnificent Buildings for his Grace the Duke of Chandos and other persons of Quality and Distinction."

He was certainly a craftsman of great versatility, able to move with apparent ease from building a humble brick box in a side street to embellishing a nobleman's mansion or even designing a theatre. What remains of his work reveals that, while in his later career he was perfectly familiar with the Palladian idiom, he always retained an eclectic attitude to style. In particular, the elaborate plasterwork which is the principal feature of his interiors derives, unsurprisingly given his early training, from a large number of sources, some of which stretch back to the vernacular traditions of the early 17th century.

In 1735, Shepherd embarked on a highly successful speculation on his own account by building Shepherd Market on the site of the ancient fairground in Mayfair. The Market House consisted of two storeys, the lower containing butchers' shops, while the upper was used as a theatre in fairtime. In March 1738, Shepherd obtained permission to hold a market for live cattle here, and at the time of his death he was stated to be the owner both of the market itself and of "many other buildings about Mayfair".

Throughout his career, he lived and worked in Mayfair and more of his work survives there today than that of any other early Georgian architect and builder. Apart from Shepherd Market and Curzon Street, he was also active in the Bishop of London's Tilney Street Estate between South Audley Street and Park Lane and on the Grosvenor Estate where he was responsible for several blocks, including houses on the north side of Grosvenor Square.

Crewe House was certainly built by Shepherd, but there is no sound evidence for the often-published belief that he lived and even died in the house. The house was unfinished at the time of his death and it is probable from entries in the ratebooks of the time that he lived latterly in a small house in the vicinity of Shepherd Market which was his major building project in his last years.

He erected the core of Crewe House, which is to say the central part between the bow-fronted wings, in 1746-7, while the wings were added later (after Shepherd's death), probably in 1753-4.

On a plan of Sir Nathaniel Curzon's estate round Curzon Street, now in the Public Records Office, a plot 60 feet wide, corresponding almost exactly to the dimensions of the existing building if the wings are excluded, is marked "Mr. Shepherd". The plan is dated 1740, but was used as a working document for several years afterwards and Shepherd's plot was drawn on at a later date. The outline plan of the house, depicted as a rectangular block, is shown on John Rocque's large-scale map of London, published in 1747, and we can guess that it was in the course of building when that section of the map was completed. (Fig. 2) In the rate books for the Out Ward of St George's Hanover Square parish compiled in December 1747, the rate collector has inserted the words "White house", at the appropriate place in the sequence of entries, but with no ratepayer's name (indicating incidentally that the house was almost

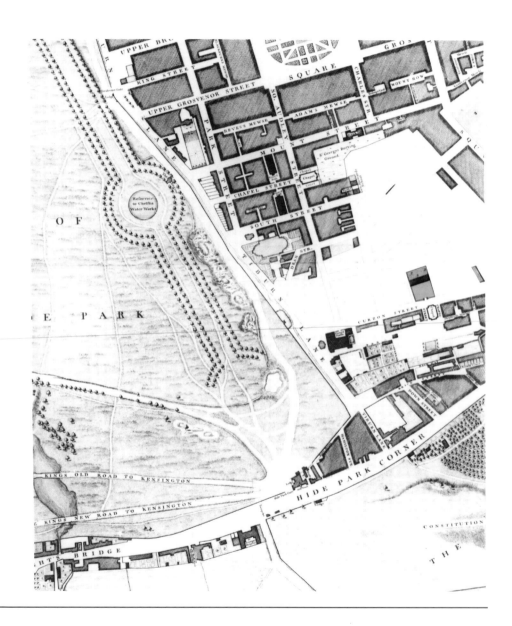

(Fig. 2.) John Rocque's Map of Mayfair, surveyed in 1747, was the most detailed map of its day. It is drawn to a scale of 26" to the mile, covering 24 sheets. The dimensions of 15 Curzon Street appear to have been determined by the size of the plot of land bought by the speculative developer Edward Shepherd, whose highly successful Shepherd Market still flourishes today on the site of the ancient Mayfair fairground.

completely stuccoed from the time of first building).

Edward Shepherd died in October 1747, "greatly lamented by all who had the Pleasure of his Acquaintance". In his will, dated 13 December 1746, he left the Shepherd Market Estate to his wife Elizabeth, who, as his executrix, was instructed to spend £300 in building an almshouse for ten poor housekeepers of the parish of St George's Hanover Square (by coincidence the church in which several members of the Crewe family of the day were married). It was to be built, "upon the ground that the lease belongs to Shepherd's Market", in accordance with a "Plan and Elevation drawn and signed by me". He also left his silver watch and an annuity of £50 to his brother, John Shepherd.

On 1st January 1748, Sir Nathaniel Curzon granted Edward Shepherd's widow Elizabeth a 999-year lease of the house and its 60-feet-wide plot. Another lease of the same date of a small plot immediately to the north states that the house was then in the possession of Richard Holmes Esquire. Holmes is entered as the ratepayer in the first ratebook for 1748 with "at Midsummer" written by his name, suggesting perhaps that he was not intending to move in until Midsummer of that year.

Holmes presumably took the house under a short-term lease or tenancy agreement with Elizabeth Shepherd as the house was almost certainly unfinished when Shepherd died. It must have been fitted out subsequently under his widow's directions for Holmes, about whom nothing is known and who, in any case, gave up the house in 1749 when it was taken by Charles, 2nd and last Viscount Fane (1708-1766), apparently still as a tenant or short-term lessee of Elizabeth Shepherd.

In June 1753, however, Sir Nathaniel gave Lord Fane a new direct 999-year lease of a very much larger plot, 132 feet 8 inches in width, in exchange for the return of Elizabeth's original lease. Fane was able and needed to obtain this because the immediate surrounding area was still

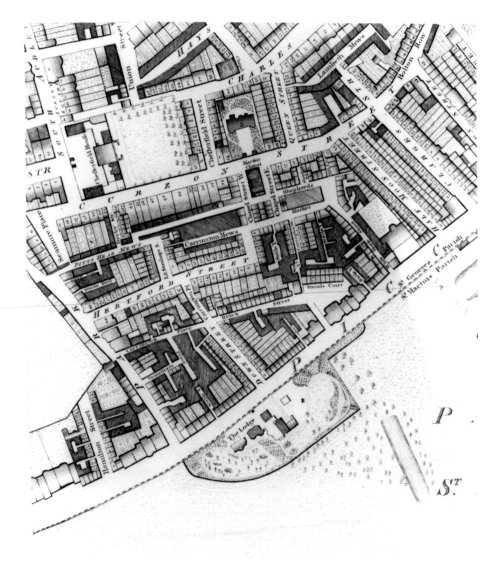

(Fig. 3) Richard Horwood's Map of Mayfair, surveyed 1792-1799, is the earliest map of London to include house numbers.

undeveloped and he was obviously contemplating enlarging the house. The plot that was granted to Fane in 1753 is precisely that of Crewe House and its grounds today.

In that same year, the rateable value of the house rose from £40 to £60 and again in 1754 from £60 to £100, which suggests that Fane enlarged the house immediately. As the value of the nearby houses remained unchanged, it is reasonable to assume that the bow-fronted wings were added in those years. It is not known who did the work, but possible candidates are John Phillips and George Shakespear, prominent mid-Georgian master-builders (Shakespear, like Shepherd, called himself an architect) who were engaged as partners in building in Curzon, Chesterfield and Queen Streets at that time.

Phillips was a party to Lord Fane's lease from Sir Nathaniel, having given up his claim to some of the land. The wings are shown in the block plan of the house on Horwood's map of 1799, the first since Rocque's map on a scale large enough to show such features. (Fig. 3)

The earliest known illustration of the house is a water-colour of 1813 by R. D. Chantrell which was drawn to accompany one of Sir John Soane's lectures and is now in the Sir John Soane Museum. (Fig. 4) The picture shows the main front of the house, although the wings are largely obscured by trees. The centre of the façade, however, is clearly depicted and one can see several features typical of Shepherd's work elsewhere, most of which have unfortunately been altered or removed. The projecting frontispiece, consisting of a heavily rusticated ground storey and superimposed columns rising through two storeys to a pediment (here shown embellished with a cartouche), is similar to those used on the north side of Grosvenor Square and at 17 Bruton Street. Other features characteristic of his work are the shell-headed openings (originally simply niches) on each side of the entrance and Gibbs surrounds to the

Venetian windows on the ground floor. Not only have these surrounds been removed in the process of simplifying and cutting down the Venetian windows, but above these windows on the upper floors two window openings have been made in place of the one provided by Shepherd for each floor. Indeed, the many alterations to the fenestration have detracted significantly from the harmony and repose of the original composition. It is only when looking at the water-colour of 1813 that one can appreciate the real quality of the design of the handsome Palladian

(Fig. 4) Façade of Lady Reade's House, by R.D. Chantrell, 1813. Mr Shepherd was primarily trained as a plasterer, which explains his use of a heavily rusticated ground storey, and the rich embellishment of the pediment.

villa that Shepherd provided for this very much altered house.

Charles Tyrrell made a ground plan of the house in 1813, also in the Sir John Soane Museum. (Fig. 5) One of the interesting features on this is an octagonal stairwell at the rear of the house, of which vestigial, structural

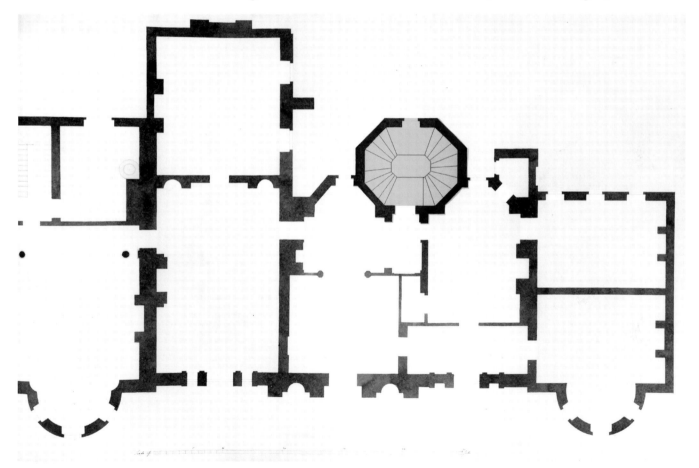

remains survive in the basement and ground floor today.

Viscount Fane's widow lived at Crewe House from 1776 till her death, aged eighty-six, in April 1792. The next occupant was Lady Reade, who took up residence the following year and lived there till her death in 1818 and is often said to have carried out some alterations to the design of Sir John Soane. But there is no evidence for this attribution, which is based on a misunderstanding of the nature of the water-colour view of the house by Soane's pupil R. D. Chantrell in the Soane Museum. This was prepared as an illustration for Soane's Royal Academy lectures on architecture and is not an architectural design by Soane himself but the equivalent of a modern colour slide. It seems clear that the substantial alteration of the house did not occur until later in the nineteenth century. Lady Reade was the wife of Sir John Chandos Reade. On her death, the lease was assigned on 27 May 1817 to Henry James Luttrell, Earl of Carhampton. But he never moved into the place, and the following year re-assigned the lease for a profit. So this transaction was probably a speculative investment, though he did start to alter the house.

Lord Carhampton was a typical Regency rake. He was a high-living eccentric who had opposed John Wilkes at the Brentford election and been bitterly satirised in the *Letters of Junius* for his pains. He was a professional soldier and Commander-in-Chief in Ireland at the time of the threat of a French invasion in the 1790s. Nathaniel Wraxall in his diaries tells a good story about him.

(Fig. 5, overleaf) Plan of Lady Reade's House, by Charles Tyrrell, 1813. Sir John Soane's use of Chantrell's water-colour and Tyrell's plan of Lady Reade's House in his Royal Academy lectures have often led to the incorrect attribution of the design of the house to Soane. Sadly virtually nothing remains of the octagonal stairwell at the rear of the house.

In 1812 soon after the restrictions imposed by parliament on the Regent were withdrawn, Lord Carhampton, lying in an apparently hopeless state at his house in Bruton Street, Berkeley Square, where he laboured under a dangerous internal malady, intelligence of his decease was prematurely carried to Carlton House. The Regent, who was at table when the report arrived, lending rather too precipitate credit to the information, immediately gave away his regiment, the Carabineers, to one of the company, a general officer, and he lost not a moment in kissing His Royal Highness's hand on the appointment. No sooner had the report reached Lord Carhampton than he instantly despatched a friend to Pall Mall, empowered to deliver a message to the Prince. In it he most respectfully protested, that far from being a dead man, he hoped to surmount his present disease, and therefore humbly entreated him to dispose of any other regiment in the service except the Carabineers. Lord Carhampton humorously added that His Royal Highness might rest assured that he would give special directions to his attendants not to lose a moment after it could be ascertained that he was really dead in conveying the news to Carlton House.

Chapter Two

Wharncliffe House

Gradually, over the century, Curzon Street became more and more fashionable. The inhabitants included such varied figures as Baron Bunsen, the Prussian ambassador in London from 1841-54, Sir Francis Chantrey, the sculptor, Madame Vestris, the popular light comedy actress, and Sir Henry Halford, a notable surgeon.

Taking 1797 at random, we find listed as resident in the street Lord Macartney, who had gone to China as George III's ambassador to the Emperor Chien Lung in Peking (accompanied, as it happened, by Lieutenant John Crewe, later the 2nd Lord Crewe and grandfather of the future owner of Crewe House). He in fact died in Curzon Street in 1806, in a small house designed by Robert Adam and described by Horace Walpole as "charming – and cheap as old clothes".

In 1818, the Hon James Stuart Wortley, a Tory MP, bought from Lord Carhampton the house built by Edward Shepherd and enlarged by Lord Fane for £12,000. It remained in his family for three generations and he re-named it Wharncliffe House when he was ennobled in 1826. Wortley was a politician of some distinction, but is perhaps best remembered today as the editor of the Works of his re-doubtable great-grandmother, the famous and somewhat cantankerous Lady Mary Wortley Montagu – traveller, letter writer and the pioneer of inoculation against smallpox.

(Fig. 6) The 1st Baron Wharncliffe (the Hon James Stuart Wortley) gave his own name to the house after he was ennobled in 1826.

James Stuart Wortley's wife, Lady Caroline, was not at first as enthusiastic about Curzon Street as she might have been. She wrote to her mother Lady Erne on 11 July 1818 to tell her the news of the purchase:

> The house in Curzon Street is ours dearest mama and a lease of 900 and odd years, which will last out many of our descendants. I am hurried and nervous with the suddenness of the decision, the more so as I hate the situation, tho' I like the House very much; and that there is an end for ever of all my dreams of a house in a Square or to the Park! But this I must try to forget, and hope I shall *grow* to like my new house, especially as the Doge is enamour'd of it. We are going there almost directly with Lord Carhampton to see what remains to be done, *he* is to finish all for painting and papering, and then *we* take it in hand . . . Don't take notice in your answer of my dislike of Curzon Street . . .

In the autumn Lady Caroline returned to London and wrote to her mother on October 12, 1818:

> If I did not want to be at home again I should completely enjoy myself here just now. My mornings are spent at the new House and shops, and my evenings at the Play.

The Stuart-Wortleys were then still in residence at their previous smaller house in Lower Brook Street while the new house was being redecorated, furnished and made ready for them to move in, which they did in Spring 1819. The main alteration to the house at this stage seems to have been the simplification of the stucco details of the exterior to give it more the character of an up-to-date Regency stucco villa. Comparison of Chantrell's view in the Soane Museum with a water-colour of *circa* 1830, formerly in the Wharncliffe collection and now the property of Mary, Duchess of Roxburghe, shows that the decorative mouldings had been removed from the pediment, the rusticated surrounds from the ground floor Venetian windows and the semi-circular pediments from the principal first floor windows. (Fig. 7) The attached columns supporting the main pediment had had their Roman Ionic capitals replaced by more fashionable Greek Ionic ones. At the same time the front door was glazed

(Fig. 7) Water-colour of 15 Curzon Street, c.1830. Following the whims of fashion Lord Wharncliffe changed the façade of 15 Curzon Street. He altered the style of the capitals from Roman to Greek Ionic, and removed the rustication and mouldings from the ground and first floor windows. Continuing his quest for the simplicity of the Greek Revival he denuded the pediment and roof cornice of their mouldings.

to let more light into the old main entrance hall. A new, more convenient, back entrance from the stable yard seems also to have been made for family use at this time. These comparatively simple alterations transformed the house's appearance from a Palladian villa to a sleek Greek Revival house, somewhat similar to those being constructed at the same time to the design of Decimus Burton in Regent's Park.

Further internal decorations were carried out by Lord and Lady Wharncliffe in 1832. Again, they are documented in the correspondence of Lady Erne (then somewhat infirm and living in a Grace and Favour apartment at Hampton Court) with her daughter while the work was in progress.

On 9 March 1832 Lady Erne wrote :

> . . . If I can get into a favorable state, I will do as you propose, & drive in some morning. I am longing as you may suppose to see you all & the Doge in his "extasies" with his house. I cannot quite make up my mind to the white walls with the pictures : yet I am quite aware of the advantages you mention, but *must I bear* with the loss of that very pretty burnt cream color in Caroline's sitting room? . . .

To which Lady Wharncliffe answered :

> . . . I am sure you will be consoled for the loss of your *burnt cream* when you see the *fresh* cream, looking so clean & light, & the pictures looking so well upon it. The difference in the light at the end of the drawing room in the morning is not to be told. But I hope you will not drive into Town to-morrow, for the two little rooms are all unfurnish'd . . . and the drawing room is not yet done. . .

The following day Lady Erne replied :

> . . . You make a very good *plaidoyer* for your creamy white, & I shall very
> likely be as much in love with it as the Doge when I come to see all its
> advantages. . .

"The Doge" was the family nickname for Lord Wharncliffe himself. He
had inherited the Wortley estates at Wharncliffe near Sheffield in
Yorkshire through a double female descent. His great-great-grandfather,
Sidney Montagu, had married the Wortley heiress. Their son in turn,
Edward Wortley Montagu, had married Lady Mary Pierrepont, daughter
of the Duke of Kingston, of Thoresby in Nottinghamshire, and had served
as a Lord Commissioner of the Treasury and ambassador to the Ottoman
Emperor in Constantinople. It was while they were in Constantinople
that Lady Mary had discovered the advantages of inoculation as a
defence against the scourge of smallpox, having her own children
vaccinated there before introducing the method into England in 1719.
Their eldest son, also Edward, was a hopeless "drop-out". He converted
to Roman Catholicism while on his Grand Tour, generally misbehaved
and died unmarried and without any legitimate children. His sister Mary,
by contrast, married the 3rd Earl of Bute, George III's earnest and
cultivated Prime Minister. Her second son, James Stuart, inherited her
Yorkshire and Cornish estates and founded the Stuart-Wortley dynasty of
Wharncliffe. It was his eldest son James, "the Doge", who bought the
Curzon Street house and was created 1st Lord Wharncliffe. The Doge was
an active Tory politician serving in successive cabinets, much involved in
the political manoeuvres surrounding the passing of the Great Reform
Bill in 1832. He was appointed Lord Privy Seal in 1834 and was the leader
of the Conservatives in the House of Lords from 1842 to 1844. Charles

Greville in his *Memoirs* described him at the time of the Reform Bill as "a very honest man, with a right view of things and a fair and unprejudiced understanding [but] vain and imprudent without authority, commanding no respect". He wrote again, more generously, after his death in 1845 :

> He was not a popular man . . . his manners were ungracious . . . but he was deservedly loved and esteemed by his family and his friends. He was kind-hearted, affectionate, hospitable and obliging, an excellent, well-meaning man. . . He was very far from being a man of first-rate capacity, but he had a good strong sense, liberal opinions, honesty, straight forwardness and courage. . . He was for above twenty years Chairman of the Quarter Sessions, and for four years Lord Lieutenant of his county [West Riding of Yorkshire] and in both capacities acted with credit and approbation. In public life thus playing a secondary, but an honorable and useful part, in private life he was irreproachable, amiable and respected . . . No man ever died with fewer enemies, with more general goodwill, and more sincerely regretted.

"The Doge" had married in 1795 the twenty-year-old Caroline "Lal-lal" Creighton, daughter of the Earl of Erne and grand-daughter of the eccentric Earl Bishop of Derry. He died having just celebrated their golden wedding. They had four children: John (2nd Lord Wharncliffe), Charles, James and Caroline. Theirs was an idyllic family life, the character of which is preserved for us in a correspondence between its different members stretching over sixty years and forming a marvellous diary of events, for the Wharncliffes were at the centre of the political and social life of their time, and their London house was a place of conviviality and generous hospitality for a wide circle of relations and friends, all known by nicknames. Lady Erne was "Gooma", grandfather

James Stuart Wortley, "Mr Pops", and the Wharncliffe children "Pusskin", "So", and "Ta". Among the groups entertained at Curzon Street was the staff of *The Owl*, the paper started by Evelyn Ashley, James Stuart Wortley and Lord Glenesk, for which Lord Wharncliffe wrote pieces. Other regular contributors included Vernon Harcourt, Lord Houghton, a Yorkshire neighbour and, curiously enough, the father of the man who would eventually buy the house from the Wharncliffes, and Samuel Wilberforce, Bishop of Oxford. Lady Wharncliffe, who outlived her husband by ten years, drew to herself the sympathy and confidence of all who knew her and formed the pivot round which revolved an exceptionally affectionate family life. The usually critical Lady Granville defined "Lal-lal's" particular charm as that of a "perfect nature, great refinement, and no wish to be anything but what she is . . . She is like a moonlight night after a hot day, refreshment and repose. She has all the charm of intelligence without the tax of 'esprit'."

Much of their year was spent in their country houses in Yorkshire, Wortley Hall, a large stone Georgian house not far from Sheffield, and Wharncliffe Lodge, an ancient hunting lodge three miles away on a crag overlooking Wharncliffe Chase, a wild and rocky moorland landscape inhabited by red deer and rabbits which had enchanted Lady Mary Wortley-Montagu, who considered the sublime view second only to that from her belvedere at Avignon. Horace Walpole, with whom she would later quarrel bitterly, had written after a visit that "the savageness of the scene would charm your Alpine taste. It is tumbled with fragments of mountains that look ready laid for building the world. One scrambles over a huge terrace on which mountain ashes and huge trees spring out of the rocks." This was just the thing to appeal to early-nineteenth century Picturesque sensibilities and the Wharncliffes adored it : "No country can possibly be wilder or more beautiful." Curzon Street seemed very tame and airless by comparison, but made an ideal base for Lord Wharncliffe's political life. He had been first elected MP for the county of York in 1818 and so needed to be in London during parliamentary sessions from then on, especially after he became a member of the Upper House, and a cabinet minister. Lady Wharncliffe soon took to Curzon Street and got much pleasure out of decorating and furnishing the house, as is made clear in her letters to her mother. "Since dinner Mr. Wortley and I have walk'd into Bond Street where we have ruined ourselves in French china and old teapots". And much else of the same vein. The house in their time, however, despite its fashionable veneer remained its mid-eighteenth century self with its main entrance still in the middle of the south front facing Curzon Street with a large drawing room and dining room (in the west wing) opening to the left, Lady Wharncliffe's sitting room situated at the back of the drawing room, and smaller rooms to the right : a morning room, and front and back libraries in the east wing. Major changes were made to the plan and layout of the rooms in the middle of the nineteenth century.

Following the 1st Lord Wharncliffe's death in 1845 the house was let to Sir Richard Sutton, a Nottinghamshire baronet made rich by the ownership of substantial London properties including Meard and Lexington Streets in Soho and much of the north side of Piccadilly. The lease to him was renewed for a further six years from April 1848 and in anticipation of that the whole house was redecorated by Fratt and Attfield at a cost of £295. The bedrooms and offices were all newly distempered and the main rooms painted and papered and their woodwork grained.

John, the 2nd Lord Wharncliffe, seems hardly to have lived in the house, it only having reverted into his vacant possession in the last year of his life. Like his father he was a moderate Conservative in politics. He married Lady Georgina Ryder, daughter of the 1st Earl of Harrowby. But his chief interest was agriculture and he spent much of his time improving his estates in Yorkshire. He died aged only 54 in 1855, and was succeeded as 3rd Lord Wharncliffe by his eldest son, Edward Montagu Stuart Wortley, who in due course was created 1st Earl of Wharncliffe (1876). He too was an active Conservative politician. He was made very rich by the industrialisation of the fringes of his estates near to Sheffield. Coal royalties, ground rents from building development and railway dividends swelled his income and augmented his agricultural rent roll. He was therefore in the position to make sweeping changes to the Curzon Street house, as well as to his seat at Wortley Hall, which he proceeded to do as soon as he inherited, for he was interested in the arts and considered himself something of a patron.

He chose as architects for the alterations the firm of William Burn (1789-1870). Burn was a prolific designer, of Scottish birth, whose reputation for good domestic planning had, by the mid-nineteenth century, won him the patronage of most of the British aristocracy. He had moved his main office from Edinburgh to Stratton Street in London in 1844 and the major business was continued there in partnership with his nephew J. MacVicar Anderson, who directed it till his own death in 1915. MacVicar Anderson seems to have been mainly in charge of the work at Curzon Street with Uncle William only being wheeled in to deal with the trickier structural problems as they arose. Burn was an architect of competence and virtuosity rather than genius. Sir Charles Barry dismissed him (no doubt with a touch of envy) as "more a man of business than an artist". Lord Wharncliffe made up for this by also appointing Frederick Cranmer Penrose, Surveyor to the Fabric of St Paul's Cathedral, to supervise the more "artistic" side of the decorations at Wortley and Curzon Street, including typically elaborate mid-Victorian

schemes of polychrome painting and stencilling. These were carried out by a firm called Pantaenius & Owen "Decorative Artists, Cabinet Makers, Uphoslterers, Painters and General Contractors of 249 Oxford Street, near Marble Arch." Sir Ambrose Poynter RA, the painter, also gave Lord Wharncliffe advice on the decorations and it was through him "that the Spanish leather wall hangings were acquired for the dining room." (Figs. 8 & 9)

(Figs. 8 & 9) It was left to Edward Montagu Stuart Wortley, 1st Earl of Wharncliffe (1876), to update the interior of the house. He redecorated the Dining Room adding the leather wall hangings.

Recent research carried out by the Guildhall Museum, London and the Colonial Williamsburg Foundation, Virginia (where the hangings are now housed), has revealed that these supposedly 'Spanish' hangings were designed and produced in England, in the late nineteenth century.

The principal alteration embarked on by Lord Wharncliffe was the complete re-orientation of the house and the removal of the main entrance from the front to the back. (Fig. 10) This no doubt made the place more comfortable, convenient and better adapted for large-scale entertainment, but spoilt the external architectural character of the house. A new carriage drive was made down the east side of the front garden and into the old stable yard at the back which now became the entrance

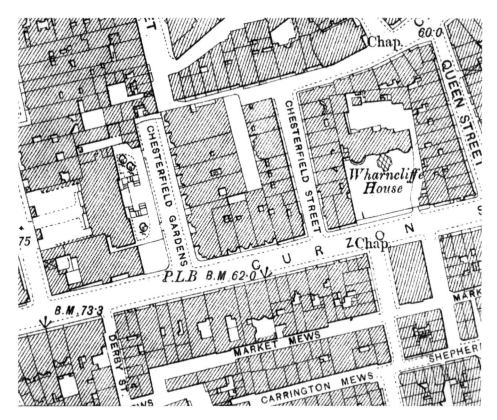

(Fig. 10) 25th Ordnance Survey of Curzon Street, 1894. With the resources gained from industrial development on the fringes of his Sheffield estates, Lord Wharncliffe reorientated the house, moving the main entrance to the rear of the house.

court. Little seems to have been done to give this side of the house a more formal character and it remained a jumble of distempered brick bays and water closet excrescences. The old drawing room was enlarged by moving its back wall into the former Lady Wharncliffe's sitting room which was halved in size. The truncated remainder was converted into a new entrance hall and lined with old oak panelling. The former entrance hall in the centre of the south front became the saloon and opening out of it, to the detriment of the façade, a large, glazed octagonal conservatory was constructed on the axis of the old front door. Though these alterations spoilt the outside, they did help to create a proper sequence of reception rooms forming an East to West enfilade from the library, boudoir or sitting room, saloon, and drawing room through to the dining room, with the conservatory providing an unexpected bonus, its bowers of scented flowers creating a perfect sitting-out place during dances in the Season. (Fig. 11)

The remodelled rooms were elaborately decorated, with gilding and "artists' work" as well as ordinary house-painting as can be deduced from the surviving bills of Pantaenius & Owen which also refer to satin wall panels, stencilled borders, and flock papers. The drawing room was heightened as well as enlarged and decorated in the French taste with a "Louis XIV" marble chimney-piece, fluted Corinthian pilasters and large looking-glasses. The library was fitted with new ebony book shelves, the bedrooms hung with chintz. In 1857 £4,334 pounds was spent on decoration and furniture, with another £4,234 the following year. Further work was done in 1861 when the saloon or music room was altered, the single connecting doors to the flanking drawing room and boudoir being replaced with wider double doors, a corner chimney-piece removed, and the wall between the saloon and boudoir properly squared off by removing a curious square cupboard-like space which had formed part of

(Fig. 11) Although the addition of the conservatory on the front of the house provided a delightful sitting-out place during dances in the Season, it was at the expense of the architectural symmetry of the façade.

the original structure of the house. These changes were masterminded by the great Mr Burn himself who wrote from Stratton Street on 10th September 1861, "I have been longer in looking at the proposed alteration in the Curzon Street house" but saw no great problems in making the change; it just involved some juggling around with iron girders to support the chimney-stack and upper walls of the house; he estimated the cost at £696. 10s. 8d. There was no quibble about this, and the alterations went ahead. The decorations in these further improved areas, including carpets and curtains, were carried out by Arthur J. Owen & Co. of Bond Street who sent in a bill of £698. 19s. 6d. for their services between 1863 and 1866.

Thereafter no major changes were made in the Wharncliffe era, but regular maintenance was carried out under the direction of MacVicar Anderson as the consultant architect (he charged 10 guineas for his work over ten years), with Messrs Smith & Co. of 9 Commercial Street, Pimlico, as the building contractors. The latter's annual accounts survive from 1875 to 1893 and give a very clear impression of the routine upkeep of an aristocratic London town house in the last part of the nineteenth century.

Regular work included repairing chimney-stacks, cleaning drains, painting the conservatory and mending furniture. The outside was repainted every 5 years, the walls and window joinery white, and the doors grained walnut. MacVicar Anderson acted for Lord Wharncliffe over any party wall negotiations with neighbours in Chesterfield Street or Queen Street who might complain about leaves from the plane trees in the front garden or even wish to open up lights in their back walls overlooking Lord Wharncliffe's property. In 1878 a new mosaic floor was laid in the entrance hall, and new cooking ranges installed in the kitchen, in 1880 electric light was installed, an early example in London. As well as what might be thought of as straightforward building work, Messrs

Smith were also responsible for special house-work such as cleaning the windows, laying carpets, or sweeping snow from the roof in winter. This is because a London house, unlike a country house, did not have a large permanent staff of its own. When the Wharncliffes came to London from Yorkshire they brought their own domestic servants with them and then took them back again. It was therefore cheaper and easier to employ an outside contractor to do all the routine maintenance and heavier work. In the same way James Veitch & Sons of the Royal Exotic Nursery in Chelsea were employed to look after the planting in the conservatory on a regular contract, rather than the Wharncliffes employing a full-time gardener of their own. When there was a large dinner party Smiths came in to set up the large table in the dining room, hung lamps and to assist with the flower arrangements, even fetching fresh flowers from Liverpool Street Station. They also "put the house to bed" and opened it up again on a regular basis when the family came to London for the Season, taking up and laying the carpets, storing or cleaning and arranging the furniture, putting out or removing dust covers, lowering or raising the window blinds, every February and August.

Throughout the 1st Earl's lifetime the Wharncliffes spent late summer, autumn and the winter at Wortley. They returned to London in February and were based there till August and the onset of grouse shooting. From February to April they lived reasonably quietly in London, just dining four or five *en famille*, but from late May to early August, during the peak of the Season, they entertained on a large scale. The Wharncliffe House cellar book survives from 1868 (when the alterations were completed and the house was ready to receive guests) till 1895, four years before the 1st Earl died. As well as recording the bottles of wine consumed (in the kitchen for cooking, as well as drunk by the family and guests in the dining room) it lists the names of all those who dined in the house every night. This is a rare and useful record of the pattern of entertainment in a large Victorian town house. In the Season the Wharncliffes gave dinner parties three times a week with between twelve and twenty people sitting down and *tout le monde* entertained : Droghedas, Cadogans, Baths, Ailesburys and all the ramifications of the, mainly Tory, aristocracy. Whigs were less frequent guests, reflecting the fact that the pattern of entertainment was mainly formed by Lord Wharncliffe's political interests and activities. This Tory phase in the history of the house ended with Lord Wharncliffe's death in 1899 and the subsequent sale of the property to a Whig family.

Chapter Three

The Crewe Era

The freehold of 15 Curzon Street – Wharncliffe House as it still remained – was put up for sale on 13th June 1901 by the auctioneer Joseph Stower of Chancery Lane, and was bought for about £90,000 by Robert Offley Ashburton Milnes, Earl of Crewe.

In April 1899, Crewe had married Lady Peggy Primrose, the younger daughter of the former Prime Minister, the Earl of Rosebery, under whose premiership Crewe had served as Viceroy of Ireland. Their wedding at Westminster Abbey had been a popular and spectacular affair, the *Evening News* even coming out on primrose coloured paper in honour of the occasion.

Crewe now wanted a house in Mayfair larger than the one in Hill Street, where he had lived after the death of his first wife. The large house in Curzon Street suited his taste for lavish entertaining.

At first he thought of calling the place Hungerford House after his grandmother Miss Walker Hungerford, the heiress to what had once been vast estates in Wiltshire, of which several thousand acres still remained in the family. However, he consulted W. A. Lindsay, Windsor Herald, at the College of Arms, who dissuaded him on the grounds that that suggested the house had once belonged to the Hungerford family. Lindsay wrote: "I think the name of a house should point either to the locality or to an owner. Before then deciding I would find out what family built or first owned the house." In the event Crewe eschewed any historical name and settled for his own title, just as the Wharncliffes had done in their time.

The choice of name seemed reasonable. He was by descent the ultimate representative of four families that had been distinguished in the legal, political, mercantile and literary life of England for at least three centuries – Crewe, Milnes, Offley as well as Hungerford.

Lord Crewe, himself, was a man of considerable abilities. An editorial in *The Nation* in 1911 commented "Lord Crewe has gifts both of temperament and intellect which approach to genius". In many ways he was an eighteenth century figure, the last of the Georgian Whigs. Like them he was rich and cultivated, with a good mind and classical education, who devoted most of his life to parliamentary and public business.

He was born in London on 12 January 1858, the only son of Richard Monckton-Milnes, 1st Lord Houghton, and Annabel Hungerford Crewe, daughter of the 2nd Lord Crewe, both of whose family inheritances were to pass to him in due course. He was educated at Harrow and Trinity College, Cambridge, where he followed his father and grandfather. At Harrow he won the poetry prize for a long piece on Gustavus Adolphus, not telling his father anything about it till he could announce his success. Lord Houghton commented : "It was very discreet of you to keep your own counsel so completely as to the poem. Nobody can now say that I wrote it!"

In London he was introduced by his father to a wide literary circle, including the elderly Thomas Carlyle, as well as to politicians. Like his father he supported the Liberals, but did not become an MP because his father died when he was only 27 and he succeeded to the Houghton peerage. Thereafter he played an active part in the House of Lords for the best part of sixty years. When Gladstone became Prime Minister (for the 4th time) in 1892, he was made Viceroy of Ireland, "the most thankless office that any human being in any imaginable community could undertake", according to John Morley, the Chief Secretary. He held his own in this difficult post, continuing under Lord Rosebery and only resigning in 1895 when the Liberal Government collapsed. He was created Earl of Crewe as a thank-you, and also a recognition of his Crewe inheritance which had come to him on the death of his uncle, the 3rd Lord Crewe, the previous year.

During Lord Salisbury's long Conservative dominance, Lord Crewe sat on the opposition front bench in the Lords for ten years. But in 1905 when the Liberals returned to power, under the premiership of Campbell-Bannerman, he was appointed Lord President of the Council and occupied a series of leading Cabinet posts over the next eleven years. In 1908 he succeeded Lord Ripon as leader of the House of Lords and was given the Garter. Asquith, who succeeded Campbell-Bannerman in the same year, made Crewe Secretary of State for Colonies and in 1910 Secretary of State for India. In that capacity he attended the Delhi Durbar, and was responsible for transferring the capital of British India from Calcutta to Delhi. When Asquith resigned in 1916, Lord Crewe went with him and never held political office again apart from a few months in Ramsay Macdonald's "National Government" in 1931. He continued to play an active public role however, serving as Chairman of the LCC from 1917 onwards, as well as being ambassador in Paris from 1922-1928. Nor were his activities narrowly political. He had a keen interest in country matters, especially farming and rural sports. He also formed a good library, and wrote several works including the official biography of his father-in-law Lord Rosebery. In 1931 he bought and restored West Horsley Place in Surrey, an ancient house with a beautiful red brick seventeenth-century façade, and it was there that he died in June 1945.

The sales particulars of Crewe House, prepared for the auction of 1901, survive and describe the property as being "of almost incomparable extent and value". (Fig. 12) They give a clear impression of the accommodation when Lord Crewe acquired the house. On the top floor there were six bedrooms and three other small bedrooms. On the first floor as well as the principal bedroom in the west wing there were two other front bedrooms, a good bedroom in the east wing, three back

bedrooms and a liberal scattering of WCs.

The main rooms on the ground floor included the entrance hall, on the north side, with a mosaic floor and the walls lined with oak panelling to a height of seven feet. (Fig. 13) The library in the east wing had a bow window and fitted ebony bookcases. "The suite of handsome reception rooms" along the south front was described in appreciative detail. The Second Drawing Room (18'10" × 17'9") was lined with satin and had carved and gilt decorations over the doors, an enriched cornice, marble chimney- piece and painted ceiling. The First Drawing Room (20'6" × 19'9"), on the site of the original entrance hall, also had a painted ceiling, gilt cornice and sculptured chimney-piece. The carved overdoors in here contained circular panels with painted landscapes. Glass doors led into the conservatory protruding from the middle of the south side of the house. The saloon, or main drawing room (29'8" × 19'6"), was described as a "noble and lofty" apartment with a carved and gilt window recess, elaborately carved and gilt chimney-piece, boldly enriched cornice and a "domed and panelled" (i.e. coved) plaster ceiling, the walls being hung with figured silk. The Dining Room in the west wing (32'6" × 19'8") balanced the library with the other bow window. It had a panelled dado of carved oak, 5'6" high, with door surrounds and a fireplace to match. The latter had an elaborately carved oak overmantel and there was also a carved oak side-board or buffet of similar character. Above the dado the walls were hung with antique embossed leather. As well as the house itself, Joseph Stower also auctioned the contents, and Lord Crewe bought some of the Wharncliffe furniture, fire irons and carpets.

The sales particulars are the best surviving record of the interior of the house as remodelled by Burn, MacVicar Anderson and Penrose for the Wharncliffe family. The range of period styles, from "Jacobean" oak in the dining room and entrance hall to Frenchy classical in the drawing

(Fig. 12 Cover & façade (overleaf) from Sales Particulars)
Described in the Sales Particulars as "one of the few remaining West-End Mansions of distinctive character . . . representing an exceptionally valuable site in the centre of the most fashionable district in London", Wharncliffe House was sold on 13th June 1901 for about £90,000.

rooms, was characteristic of Victorian decoration in Mayfair where a balance between masculine dark woods in the dining room and library and feminine silk and gilt in the drawing rooms was almost a convention. To Lord Crewe, all this sombre, elaborate decoration seemed old-fashioned and gloomy; he wished to restore the house to its original Georgian grace and elegance, albeit on a rather grander note than anything the house had ever known in the eighteenth century itself.

J. T. Wimperis & Arber, Architects, supervised works of redecoration immediately after Lord Crewe's purchase; what they called "cleaning and getting the place fit for your occupation". The returns of the District Surveyor for the parish of St George Hanover Square chart the further alterations to the house during Lord Crewe's occupancy. The first stage seems to have involved the modernisation of the practical side of the house. In 1902, for instance, a bathroom was constructed adjoining the

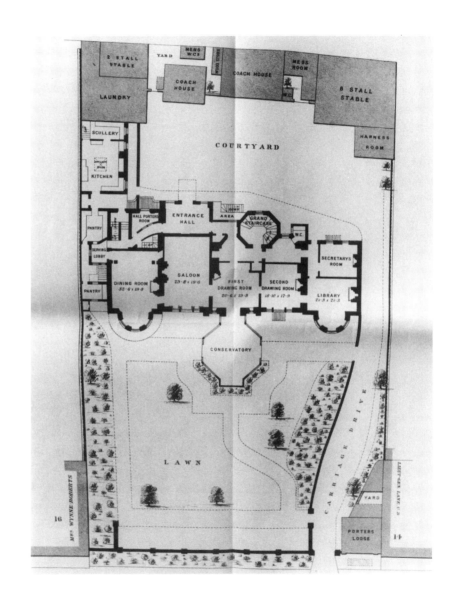

(Fig. 13) As noted by the surveyors the development prospects of the site of Crewe House where immense: "The Property occupies a frontage of about 130 feet, extends to an average depth of 220 feet, and contains an area of about 29,500 superficial feet, and, either as at present utilized, or for the erection of a more important Mansion sufficient to meet the demands of a large establishment, or by any further development of its capabilities, it represents a site of almost incomparable extent and value."

principal bedroom, by the builders W. Johnson & Co. Ltd.

Much internal redecoration was done over the following years, the oak work and leather wall hangings in the dining room and the dark ebony bookcases in the library being removed. The old stamped Spanish leather from the dining room was sold by Lord Crewe to Partridges, the well-known antique dealers, who acquired it on behalf of a museum. In 1909 a new Georgian style drawing room was added at the back of the house, and called the North Room. The builders of this extension were Spencer Santo & Co. and the decorators who designed and superintended the work were the well-known firm of Keeble & Co. It seems likely that Keebles were responsible for all the internal decoration carried out by Lord and Lady Crewe at Crewe House during these years. They are among a group of leading firms of decorators who were kept nearly continuously employed as architectural improvers in Mayfair throughout the Edwardian period on schemes of almost reckless extravagance and panache, whose opulence was only matched by their transitoriness. The period from the 1890s until the 1920s saw the fashionable heyday of elaborate interior decoration in London houses. Many firms, some of them still in business, like Maples, White Allom, Green & Abbot, Lenygon & Morant or Turner Lord of Mount Street, all came to prominence during this era. Keeble & Co., later Keeble Brothers Ltd. of Grosvenor Street, were typical of these firms in that they were antique dealers as well as architectural decorators. They were among the pioneers of fashionable Georgian revival in England; their work being scholarly and redolent of discerning taste. They were responsible for many now lost schemes in Mayfair including the lavish interior of Lord Nunburnholme's house at 41 Grosvenor Square (recorded in photographs by Bedford Lemère, 1926) or the neo-Georgian interior of 22 South Audley Street created in 1902-3 in association with Detmar Blow.

(Fig. 14) The Red Drawing Room, 1908.
Edwin Beresford Chancellor's Private Palaces of London, 1908,
provides an invaluable record of the house before the fire of 1911.
The coved ceiling was decorated in gold and the walls lined in
satin finished with carved and gilt decorations.

The rooms at Crewe House, as first redecorated and furnished by Lord
Crewe, are described in some detail by Edwin Beresford Chancellor in his
Private Palaces of London, Past and Present published in 1908. Chancellor
was enthusiastic about the spacious setting, which has always been an
attraction, and admired "the plane trees that embower Crewe House . . .
in summer, when the sun glints through their thick foliage and casts a
thousand chequered shadows on the ground." Lord Crewe had filled the
house with excellent family paintings and furniture as well as

redecorating the rooms to make a suitable setting for these heirlooms. Much of the arrangement of the things seems to have been supervised by Lady Crewe, who inherited from her mother a fine eye for such details. (Fig. 14) Beresford Chancellor found the results impressive and gave a very full description of their appearance:

> Like all large houses in London, Crewe House is filled with artistic treasures, and although there are many which have an historic *provenance*, the greater number have a claim to notice as being family heirlooms, which gives them an added interest. Considering what a large space Lord Crewe's father – the Monckton-Milnes, Lord Houghton, of an earlier day – occupied in the social, political, and literary life of his times, it would be strange if we did not find, in this house, a wealth of reminiscences of that remarkable man, and here in the Entrance Hall hangs his portrait by Rudolph Lehmann, while in the Drawing Room, the windows of which look out on to the garden over whose walls the Duke of Marlborough's stately stone residence rears its ample proportions, hang a number of portraits of the forbears of that most literary of peers. (Fig. 15)
>
> Here are Sir Robert Milnes and his wife – Lady Milnes, daughter and co-heir of Joseph Poole of Drax Abbey – in full length, by Romney [the painting of Lady Milnes now hangs in the Frick Museum in New York]; and close by, Mrs. Cunliffe Offley, by Sir Thomas Lawrence; the dog which she nurses being from the hand of Landseer; an earlier portrait of the same lady, when yet Miss Emma Crewe, is by Hoppner; and the portrait of her husband, Mr. Cunliffe Offley, by Harlow, hangs on the opposite wall. Two more noticeable family portraits are those of John, first Lord Crewe, and his wife Frances, Lady Crewe, daughter of Fulke Greville, of Wilbury, Wilts., by Lawrence; a beautiful portrait of Madame Rodes, by Gainsborough, a picture of a young boy, entitled 'Edwin', by

Wright of Derby, and two landscapes by Zuccarelli, complete the pictorial decoration of the Drawing Room, in which French furniture and *bric-à-brac*, lighted up by two mirrors, one of which hangs over the mantelpiece, in elaborately carved and gilded frames, giving a touch of Italy to the apartment which the deeply moulded ceiling dominates.

(Fig. 15) Red Drawing Room fireplace, 1908.
The richly moulded ceiling and the elaborately carved and gilded frames of the mirrors are typical of the heavy Italianate style fashionable in the later half of the nineteenth century. The chimney-piece was richly decorated with gilt ornament.

(Fig. 16) The Boudoir could be entered from the garden. The walls, lined with light blue silk panels, were hung with family miniatures and old theatrical prints and bordered with holly-pattern relief mouldings. The delicacy of the room was reflected in the cupids and medallions of baskets of flowers carved over the doors, and the ceiling painted with cupids representing the four seasons in oval medallions at each corner.

(Fig. 17) Lord Crewe redecorated the Dining Room, removing the antique embossed leather, to maximise the natural light source created by the semi-circular bay window. The walls are in white ornamental panel work with carved wood mouldings, the dado carved in relief with flowers, fruit and shells. This room was to become part of the Drawing Room.

From this Drawing Room two other apartments are reached, opening into each other, and forming one of the delightful vistas which are so pleasant a feature in many of the larger London houses. The Boudoir, seen through an intervening apartment known as the Central Drawing Room, in which hangs Romney's speaking portrait of Miss Hannah Milnes, and from which opens an octagonal winter garden. The Boudoir, with its Louis Quinze and Louis Seize furniture, and its peaceful outlook on to the gardens, is, indeed, one must think, named on the same *lucus a non lucendo* principle on which Lord Chesterfield once said his similarly called room at Chesterfield House was. (Fig. 16) Miniatures of members of both Lord and Lady Crewe's family, old theatrical prints, *bijouterie*, and the thousand and one costly trifles that help to furnish a room, are here; and here, too, is a marvellous writing-table in marqueterie, the work of the great André Boulle.

There are, too, several pictures of great interest in this room, among which I must particularly note a small but very fine portrait of Miss Emma Crewe by Gainsborough, and a portrait of Fanny Burney by Downman, by whom there is another head of a young girl, not improbably, though the fact is not stated, one of the numerous portraits of the ladies of the Crewe family, which the artist is known to have executed during the year 1777. There is, besides, a noticeable portrait of Lord Chesterfield, as well as 'Le Jardin d'Amour', by Rubens, a small copy or possibly a replica of the celebrated picture now in the Prado, which Philip IV of Spain caused to be hung in his bedroom; and there is also Clarkson Stanfield's 'Bridge of Angers', among other works which help to beautify the room.

From the Boudoir one enters the Library, which until recently was rather sombre with its black ebony bookcases and dark wall-paper, but which has now been converted into a bright, almost gay, room. The relatively few books here are chiefly those required for reference and official work, Lord Crewe's fine Library being at Fryston, but there are two pictures of peculiar interest in this room; one is the portrait of John Keats at Wentworth Place, seated and holding a book, by Severn, another example of which is in the National Portrait Gallery; the other, Stone's drawing of Rogers, Mrs. Norton, and Mrs. Phipps, sitting talking round a table; and the three-quarter-length portrait of Miss Annabel Crewe, afterwards Lady Houghton, mother of the present Lord Crewe, by Sir William Boxall, has an intrinsic interest in this house, although as a work

(Fig. 18) *The Steward's Room, 1908.*
Crewe House had extensive servants' quarters including the
steward's room, the housekeeper's room, servants' hall, butlers'
pantry, housemaids' room, chefs' room and six servants'
bedrooms.

(Fig. 19) *Bedroom Chimney-piece, 1908.*
On the first floor there were six principal bedrooms and two
bathrooms, with a further six secondary bedrooms and one
bathroom on the second floor, excluding the servants' quarters.
All the bedrooms faced the front garden and were fitted with
stoves and chimney-pieces.

of art it can only be considered as mediocre.

The Dining Room on the west side of the house is a similar room to the Library, but much longer. (Fig. 17) Two pillars support the ceiling at the back of the room; and here again, as in the Library, a change of decorative note has largely improved the lighting and general appearance of the apartment, which was formerly panelled with a dado in rich dark oak, and possessed a sideboard of massive proportions and other decorations *en*

suite; now, however, white is the prevailing tone, and an air of lightness has been given to the room which has greatly added to its charm. Among the pictures which hang here, is a portrait of George Canning, as a young man, by Hickey, and George, Prince of Wales, by Hoppner; and there is an interesting work by Stubbs representing R. S. Milnes, Esq., M.P., on horseback, although it is the two Romney portraits of the first Lord Crewe, and of Mrs. Shore Milnes, that will chiefly attract the lover of the beautiful in art.

It is clear from this long description that the layout was still the same as in the Wharncliffe period with the entrance to the north, and the conservatory or winter garden still obscuring the south front. Lord Crewe's major change was to reverse this and to restore the original layout, by demolishing the conservatory and recreating the main entrance on the south side. The builders Rice & Sons of Stockwell were carrying out these alterations when a serious fire broke out in the early hours of 10th February 1911. Thanks to the efforts of the fire brigade, the blaze was restricted mainly to the second floor; but it resulted in the destruction of most of the roof as well as causing water and smoke damage to the rooms below; in the clear light of day the blackened remains presented a most melancholy spectacle. *The Times* noted in passing that the scene "was rendered the more miserable by the fact that the front courtyard was filled with builders 'plant'" (the structure of the building still has traces of the fire damage in the form of charred beams today). Lord Crewe, himself, was philosophical about the disaster. "It might have been a lot worse," he is reported to have said. "I have been going to alter the place for some time past, and had just made arrangements to do so. This is an opportunity that is perfectly unique."

Additional drama was lent to the event by the fact that Lady Crewe had just given birth to a son that night. She and the baby had to be hastily evacuated from the blazing house to Lord Rosebery's residence nearby. Lady Crewe later described the fire in a foreword to James Pope-Hennessy's biography of her husband, *Lord Crewe 1858-1945 : The Likeness of a Liberal,* (published in 1955):

> The fire at Crewe House was indeed dramatic and merits a description in greater detail. It broke out almost simultaneously with the birth of my son – I think about midnight. It raged, and for a time there was a fear that the trees in front of the house would catch fire, and that would have made it difficult to leave or save the house. I was always told that fourteen fire-engines were employed. Happily, all was subdued, and in the early hours of the morning, my child and I were taken in an ambulance to my father's house, number 38 Berkeley Square. The strain on my husband was great, and it was due no doubt to this and other anxieties that, a short time after, he was brought back unconscious from the Pricking of Sheriffs' Dinner at Claridge's by John Burns, and for a time my father's house became a sort of hospital.

Contemporary newspapers mingled commiserations on the fire with congratulations on the birth.

Lord Crewe, himself, alluded to the fire in his deprecating, understated manner in a letter to a political colleague, Lord Hardinge:

> You must forgive a very brief letter from me this week which to me has not erred in the direction of the commonplace: On Tuesday night Peggy's boy was born. The event is the greatest possible joy to us, I need not tell you. Then our house caught fire, from the old story, I think, of joists running under a hearthstone, a place which always gets you sooner

or later. It was not an agreeable moment, with what appeared to be the certain prospect of having to move Peggy to nowhere in particular at 1 in the morning. But this was staved off and she showed great pluck and coolness.

Though Lord Crewe thought the fire was caused by a joist under a hearthstone, other sources attributed the fire, which broke out upstairs in the west wing, to an electric wire fusing. At the height of the blaze fourteen engines and a hundred firemen fought the flames. The Crewes stayed at Lord Rosebery's house in Berkeley Square until Crewe House had been reroofed and the interior repaired. The chief advantage of the fire was that it made possible the construction of an impressive two-storeyed hall in the centre of the south front, a high vaulted plaster ceiling being constructed in the place of the burnt out upper rooms there; and this hall remains the chief internal architectural feature of the building today. A plain, square stuccoed porch was added, and a gravelled semi-circular carriage sweep laid out, approached from a pair of new gates at either end of the iron railings dividing the garden from Curzon Street. (Fig. 20) Further internal alterations carried out at this time include the enlargement of the drawing room by knocking down the dividing wall between it and the dining room to create one spacious, but rather amorphous, reception room, recorded in a sketch by Hanslip Fletcher. (Fig. 21) A large new dining room was made at the back of the west wing which could seat up to a hundred people at small round tables. These rooms were embellished with Georgian-style plasterwork and brought-in marble chimney-pieces of high quality. The architects for this final phase of work were Elms and Jupp. The house remained as remodelled by Lord Crewe in 1911 till it was sold in 1937. Little work was carried out after the last World War.

(Fig. 20 overleaf) Hanslip Fletcher was commissioned to draw Crewe House in 1936. When it was put up for sale it was assumed by many that the site would be bought by a developer, and the house demolished.

(Fig. 21 overleaf) Drawing Room, by Hanslip Fletcher, 1936. Having extended the rear of the house to accommodate a new Dining Room, Lord Crewe integrated the former Saloon and Dining Room to form this extensive Drawing Room.

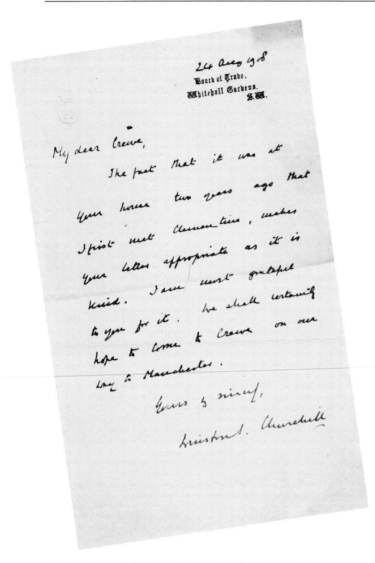

(Fig. 22) A Letter from Winston Churchill, aged 34, to Lord Crewe, 24 August 1908, tells of a crucial encounter.

During Lord Crewe's occupation, the old house became once more very much the home of a family although, through force of circumstances, there were many occasions when the Crewes had to leave it for a time. There were all the natural events of family life – birth, death, weddings, tragedy and happiness.

Sadly the son, Jack, Earl of Madeley, born on the night of the fire, was brought home from school in 1922, suffering from a severe mastoid infection. He died within a few days in a room overlooking Curzon Street.

There were many happier events. In March 1915, Lady Crewe had a daughter, Mary, also born in the house. The Crewes' style of entertaining was lavish, even by Edwardian standards. After they left Crewe House, for the comparatively modest Argyll House in the Kings Road, when one might have expected slightly reduced standards, James Pope-Hennessey wrote that dining there "provided a spectacle of almost historical interest, with the table laden with gold plate, and attended by several footmen".

One may imagine how much more sumptuous it was at Crewe House before the First World War, when, for instance, Edward VII came, as he often did, for dinner. Crewe, indeed, is said to have been the last man to have had powdered footmen behind each chair.

It was at a ball at Crewe House at that time that Winston Churchill first met his future wife. Replying to Lord Crewe's letter of congratulations on his engagement to Clementine Hozier (Fig. 22), he wrote:

My dear Crewe,

The fact that it was at your house two years ago that I first met Clementine, makes your letter appropriate as it is kind. I am most grateful to you for it. We shall certainly hope to come to Crewe on our way to Manchester.

Yours sincerely

Winston S. Churchill

In 1958, Lady Churchill wrote to Lady Crewe:

I am thrilled that you remember that it was in your house that Winston and I first saw each other. I remember the exact spot in the Ball Room.

Family life at Crewe House was interrupted by the 1914-18 war. With typical, patriotic generosity Lord Crewe, who had been made a Marquess in 1911, put the house at the disposal of the government. It was taken over by the new Ministry of Propaganda under the direction of Lord Northcliffe and "Crewe House" came to be synonymous with the Allies' propaganda efforts in the First World War. Viscount Northcliffe, the newspaper tycoon, accepted the Prime Minister, Lloyd George's invitation to become Director of Propaganda in February 1918 and took over Crewe House as his office. There he built up an organisation staffed by military and foreign office officials, academics and others all deeply versed in foreign politics, with an understanding of the different enemy countries. Their aim was to reveal to the enemy the hopelessness of his cause and the inevitability of the Allied victory and thus to undermine his moral resistance. Lord Northcliffe set up at Crewe House a committee of well-known men of affairs and publicists to advise on the conduct of the propaganda campaign. The members of the committee were:

Colonel the Earl of Denbigh	Sir Sidney Low
Robert Donald	Sir Charles Nicholson
(then Editor of the *Daily Chronicle*)	James O'Grady
Sir Roderick Jones	H.F. Wells
(Managing Director of Reuter's Agency)	H.K. Hudson (Secretary)
H. Wickham Steed	
(Foreign Editor and later Editor-in-Chief of *The Times*)	

Sir Campbell Stuart was appointed Deputy Director of the department and Deputy Chairman of the Committee. The department was divided into two main branches, the one for production, and the other for distribution, of propaganda material. In its turn the production branch was divided into German, Austro-Hungarian, and Bulgarian sections.

Activities were directed first against the Austro-Hungarian empire which was especially susceptible to propaganda as the different nationalities, Poles, Czecho-Slovaks, Slavs, and Rumanians offered a receptive condition for arousing hostility to the war effort of the Hapsburgs and Imperial Germany.

The production of propaganda literature at Crewe House, and its distribution were planned as different functions, performed by different sections of the department. The distribution to the German and Bulgarian troops was undertaken by the British Army, while distribution of propaganda to Austro-Hungarian troops was the responsibility of the Italian army. Distribution through civil channels was conducted via groups specially set up in different parts of Europe. All this work was co-ordinated by daily meetings of liaison officers and the departments at Crewe House. Leaflets were prepared and printed and then scattered over enemy lines and territory from aeroplanes or balloons. The effectiveness of Crewe House contribution to the Allied war effort was attested at the time by tributes in German newspapers:

"In propaganda the enemy is undoubtedly our superior" (Berlin *Morgenpost*). "At any rate the British Propaganda Department has worked hard. Had we shown the same activity in our Propaganda perhaps many a thing would have been different now" *(Rheinische-Westfälische-Zeitung).* "We Germans have a right to be proud of our General Staff. We have our feeling that our enemies' General Staff cannot hold a candle to it, but we also have the feeling that our enemies have a brilliant Propaganda General Staff, whereas we have none" *(Deutsche Taganzeitung).* Lord Northcliffe's achievement was to take the lessons learnt from building up the mass-populist press in England and to apply them in the context of modern warfare to undermine the enemy's morale.

Sir Campbell Stuart, who served as deputy to Lord Northcliffe at Crewe House, published a history of the Propaganda campaign masterminded on the premises, which was published in 1920 and entitled *Secrets of Crewe House.* Lord Crewe objected to the name of the book on the grounds that it "sounds more like a record of social scandal than of public work" and had suggested the alternative "Crewe House in War Time" but he did not press this point and Campbell Stuart stuck to his original title.

The propaganda mission at Crewe House was wound up at the end of 1918, after the Allied victory. The building was then handed over to another government department for a short time before being returned to Lord Crewe. Its unique role in 1918, and the contribution of the propaganda activities carried on within its walls to the Allied Victories gave the house a distinctive niche in modern English history. As Sir Campbell Stuart put it : "Crewe House will always be remembered for its propaganda politics for which, as has been truly said, it became as well

(Fig. 23) Amongst Lord Crewe's extensive alterations to the house was the restoration of the façade to its original arrangement. The conservatory was removed and the entrance returned to the south front.

known in the Chancelleries of Europe as it had been in Great Britain for so long as a social centre for national politics."

The Crewes did not stay long after they regained their home. There was

(Fig. 24) Lady Crewe, formerly Lady Peggy Primrose, drawn by John Singer Sargent, the most fashionable portrait artist of the day.

(Fig. 25) Lord Crewe, by Leon Bakst, 1921 – in fact, one of the sketches for Bakst's designs for The Sleeping Beauty in which the artist used the friends of his sponsor, Lord Rothschild, as models.

the distress of the death of their son and it may have been something of a relief to get away when Crewe was appointed ambassador in Paris, where he remained until 1928.

During those years, the house was let first to the fashionable hostess Mrs Corrigan and then as a residence for two successive American ambassadors in London – Frank Billings Kellog, who was ambassador until 1925 and then Alanson Bigelow Houghton, and who had a young daughter for whom he gave grand dances; he stayed until 1928.

However, when the Crewes came home life picked up very much where it had left off. The entertaining resumed on the same generous scale as before. Their daughter Mary was growing up and her friends remember that visits to the house were, for young people, awesome experiences at which they were banished to the furthest end of the dining room. Mary had her coming-out dance at the house in 1933. Lord Crewe's granddaughter, Mary O'Neill and Mr Derick Gascoigne (the parents later of Bamber Gascoigne) had their wedding reception there in April 1934.

In 1935 Lady Mary Crewe-Milnes married the Duke of Roxburghe, like her parents in Westminster Abbey. The reception, to which Queen Mary came, was naturally at Crewe House.

Lord Crewe had, since being briefly Minister of War in 1931, played a much smaller part in the political life of the country. The entertainments at Crewe House became more private. He also opened the house on occasion for special groups. In 1936, for instance, shortly before he sold the house, the National Art Collections Fund organised a visit to see the family portraits and other works of art. It was the swan-song for the house, for a year later it passed out of private hands forever.

Chapter Four

Conversion to Offices for Thomas Tilling

The years after the end of the Great War witnessed what *The Times* called "an orgy of destruction" as mansion after mansion fell to the pickaxe. Devonshire House in Piccadilly, with its three-acre garden, went in 1920. The beautiful mahogany doors from the house were bought by Harold Macmillan's mother for Birch Grove, the house she was building in Sussex. Lansdowne House, a couple of hundred yards from Crewe House had become a club. Of the original building, only one room with a fine coved ceiling was preserved.

Londonderry House was also a club, but was later to follow the fate of two other splendid Park Lane houses, Dorchester House and Grosvenor House, which were pulled down to be replaced by hotels. Chesterfield House, almost a next-door neighbour to Crewe House disappeared in 1933.

Crewe House, with its friendly lawns, large garden and stable yard, must have been a tempting sight to developers. Yet it stood out, almost alone in its splendour. There had, in fact as early as 1908, been a rumour that it might be sold for redevelopment. Beresford Chancellor (see p. 51) reported:

> As I write there is an attempt to sell Crewe House, with its gardens extending to an area of over 19,000 square feet; and as the particulars tell me, comprising the choicest site in Mayfair, and one of the most important in the west-end. Should the old house and its unique grounds pass into the hands of some one buying it as a residence, all will be well; but if, as is more likely when we look round and see what has happened in analogous cases – in that of Harcourt House, for instance – the property is purchased for building development, then we may expect one day in the near future to see palatial flats dominating this spot and perhaps equalling in solidity, and more than equalling in size, Sunderland House

opposite. In this case what has been here set down about Crewe House will, I hope, serve to recall its past outlines, and the interest of its contents to those to whom it has for long been a landmark, and to those who have so often gathered together within its hospitable walls.

Nothing is so difficult to remember as the appearance of a building that has been demolished; the mind, apparently, is so much more capable of receiving new impressions than of retaining old ones; and it is for this reason that any attempt to preserve the features of some building which is likely to become the victim of time's destroying hand, contributes something to the rehabilitation of the ever-changing features of our great city.

Lord Crewe had put the house on the market in February 1908, and sales particulars had been printed by Farebrother, Ellis, Egerton Beard & Co. for what they called "the choicest site in Mayfair". The house failed to meet its reserve and was bought in at £100,000.

Happily, the house was to survive for another three decades in private hands, by which time there was a very different prevailing spirit. The tide had turned strongly in favour of architectural preservation and against the spate of uncontrolled demolition that robbed London of so much fine eighteenth-century architecture. The Georgian Group, for instance, was founded in 1937, the year that Crewe House finally passed out of private hands, specifically to save Georgian buildings, parks and gardens from destruction or disfigurement. It was this new mood that helped to ensure that Crewe House was not demolished by any speculator.

Lord Crewe had always had extravagant tastes but, by the 1930s, it was time for retrenchment. He had already sold a great deal. The Romney of Mrs Milnes had gone, largely to pay for his six very expensive years as ambassador in Paris. His father's lands in Yorkshire had gone and, in

1933, he sold the bulk of his 20,000 acres in Cheshire, including Crewe Hall, to the Duchy of Lancaster, typically for far less than it was worth, on the grounds that the Crown would look after the tenants better.

Now, it was the turn of his London house, which even he could see was an anachronism. Soon after he moved to Argyll House in the King's Road in Chelsea, where the *ancien régime* splendour was not altogether forgotten, Lord Crewe's biographer describes visiting the family:

> . . . here up to the outbreak of the Second World War, they would entertain in an ample, old-fashioned way which seemed to one very young man when he dined there to provide a spectacle of almost historical interest, with the table laden with gold plate, and attended by several footmen.

Crewe House was bought by Thomas Tilling Ltd., a large and successful public company, to serve as its headquarters. The firm of Thomas Tilling was primarily a bus company, but had also branched out into construction work. Thomas Tilling, the founder of Thomas Tilling Ltd., came to London in 1847. Starting with one horse, he founded a successful firm of job masters in Peckham, south London, hiring out horses and carriages for weddings and other private functions. In 1851 he was the first to operate a horse bus service between fixed points – Peckham to Oxford Circus and back – at fixed times at a fixed fare. Other routes followed. Upon Thomas Tilling's death the business had 2,500 horses and by the turn of the century 6,000 horses, with the original job master function still the mainstay of business. Motor buses began to replace the horse buses in 1904, the year that Thomas Tilling became a public company, Tilling being the first of the established bus companies to begin the transition to motor power.

Thomas Tilling's decision to transfer from its old office in Victoria

Street to Crewe House was a remarkable gesture, rare at that time, and owed much to the vision of the chairman, Sir Frederick Heaton. With hindsight it seems extraordinary that more of the fine Georgian houses of Mayfair were not converted to "prestige headquarters" between the Wars, as was the case with many architecturally distinguished buildings in Paris and Rome. Some like Spencer House or Harcourt House became clubs, but apart from Crewe House only the Williams-Wynne house (by Robert Adam) in St James's Square was sensitively converted to a headquarters, by the National Distillers' Company, in the 1930s. This seems particularly strange as a large London house adapted well to this function, the grand reception rooms making splendid boardrooms, directors' dining rooms and offices for senior staff, while the capacious back areas provided plenty of space for more utilitarian offices.

Thomas Tilling spent six months adapting Crewe House between its purchase and moving in in November 1937. They used their own in-house architect and surveyor, H. J. Starkey, A.I.A.S., for the work. The façade was kept much as it was, except two new windows were inserted on either side of the pedimented centre, to replace the original single window in this position. This affected the proportions of the façade somewhat but was reasonably tactfully done, an effort being made "to match the existing". (Fig. 26) At the same time, the lodges and brick wall to Curzon Street were demolished and replaced by an iron railing, thus opening up the garden to the view of the passer-by. The main rooms retained much of their old character. The Boudoir became the Directors' Dining Room, the North Room the Board Room and the Yellow Drawing Room the office of the Group Managing Director. The upper floors were subdivided to make smaller offices and the old kitchen area and stables at the back reconstructed to provide additional space. The work was much admired at the time. A journalist wrote:

Even passers-by have reason to feel grateful for the admirable taste with which the house has been adapted to its new purpose. The front façade has been left untouched except for a new coat of paint and the inscription of Thomas Tilling, Limited, in gold lettering above the portico. The alteration of the entrance, the removal of one or two trees and lodges, together with the lowering of the wall, enable people to appreciate something of the classical elegance of the house.

Crewe House has had many distinguished owners in the past – Mr Shepherd, who built the house and gave his name to the market opposite; Lord Wharncliffe, a prominent politician at the time of the Reform Bill; and more lately Lord Crewe. Yet it seems to have adapted itself quite naturally to the members of the commercial organization whom it now shelters. Great credit is due to the architect and officials for the speed at which they worked to change the building within seven months from a private house to an office. The original fireplaces and the moulded ceilings have been preserved, though where a room has of necessity been divided the moulding has been carefully copied for the new wall. As is certainly inevitable and doubtless deserved, the best and largest room is given to the directors, and there can be few more distinguished board-rooms in London. This was the ballroom of the old house.

The Yellow Room, where only last year Lord and Lady Crewe held a big reception for the Liberal Party, has been cut in half for offices. Out of the North Room, dining-rooms have been made, one for the directors and the other for the senior officials of the company.

It has only been possible to keep so many of the characteristic features of the house by taking full advantage of the stables and back premises, where what may be called the main bulk of the staff is housed. The decorations throughout are light and cheerful. There are few pictures, though the directors take their luncheon opposite a painting of the Grand Canal at Venice – a peculiar choice for those whose principal concern is with roads. There are also portraits of the founder of the firm and his son, from the artistic point of view perhaps hardly worthy successors to the magnificent portraits of Master Crewe and Mrs Crewe by Sir Joshua Reynolds, but in the new character of the house appropriate and not without dignity.

(Fig. 26) Thomas Tilling's adaptation of Crewe House from a family house to functional offices was carried out with a sympathetic appreciation for the existing building. The fenestration of the façade was altered, but the overall design remained virtually untouched.

The Times devoted an editorial to the conversion on Monday, 8 November 1937, where it set aside its prejudice against office conversions and praised Thomas Tilling for its imaginative and far-sighted choice of new headquarters and adaptation of an historic building.

CREWE HOUSE TODAY

There appears on another page a description of Crewe House in its new role as commercial premises. After the orgy of destruction that has gone on during the last fifteen years among the historic houses of London the uppermost feeling in people's minds must be one of thankfulness that Crewe House still stands. It is true that the largest rooms, like the political party which was often entertained in them, have suffered a diminution in size. The masterpieces of REYNOLDS's brush have given place to pictures of Victorian commercial potentates, and peace and quiet have fled before the rattle of typewriters and a carillon of telephone bells. Yet from the outside the front of the house looks its old familiar self. Indeed the alterations to the entrance enable it to be even better seen by the passer-by. No doubt this façade hides a warren of offices on the site of the old stables and back premises, but from the aesthetic point of view that need cause no disturbance.

It is greatly to be hoped that the remaining large houses of London, like Apsley House and Bath House, will long remain in private occupation. There seems to be an impression that the "luxury flats" which have swallowed up several of these London houses have met the public demand, and a large family mansion (to use a phrase from the estate agent's vocabulary) is seldom suited for conversion into business premises. Without worrying overmuch at an old sore, it may be remembered that the conversion of part of Carlton Gardens into a business house found few defenders. No doubt the comparatively large area on which Crewe House stood made it especially suitable for enlargement into commercial premises. There can be no doubt that the most successful purpose to which these houses can be put, after they pass from private ownership, is for conversion into clubs or similar institutions. LORD HARCOURT's old house, which is now the Savile Club, is an admirable example of this. The folly of destroying buildings of historic or architectural value merely to satisfy a fashionable lust for tenement life is being realized by increasing numbers of people and has been constantly urged in these columns. The knowledge that Crewe House – in its essentials at least – has been preserved by an old-established and respected firm gives confidence for the future.

Crewe House escaped damage in the Second World War and continued to serve satisfactorily as company offices for Thomas Tilling in the 1940s and 1950s. The house was listed as a building of special architectural or historic interest in 1958. The Tilling Group enjoyed considerable expansion in the wake of the post-war construction boom. This made the old buildings an increasingly tight fit. In 1960, it was decided, therefore, to build a large new office block at the back of the site, stretching right through to Hill Street. The old house was kept much as it was, but the staircase was removed to make way for a new circulation space, lifts and new staircase in the link between the old and new buildings. The North Room was demolished at the same time and replaced by a new board room, in which the Georgian marble chimney-piece supplied by Keebles' for Lord Crewe was re-used.

The new building was a plain rectangular block with a steel-frame and flat roof. It rose two storeys higher than old Crewe House, but the top was treated with a stucco finish and cornice, so that from Curzon Street it looked like a recessed attic storey. The interior of the new block comprised utilitarian open-plan office space. The architects for all this work were the commercial firm of Gunton & Gunton who had designed many of the post-war office blocks (neither traditional nor modern) built in the City in the 1950s. Further minor internal works were carried out by Thomas Tilling to the design of Trehearne & Norman in 1981.

The occupation of the house by a large commercial organisation, over a long period, inevitably had a dispiriting effect on the appearance of Crewe House. Modern light fittings, gloss paint, linoleum and net curtains reduced the quality of the rooms. The construction of the large new office block at the back reduced the old house to a mere overture. The façade, however, survived and was always splendidly maintained by the Thomas Tilling Group, freshly painted in bright cream, while the lawns in front of the house were kept in immaculate, bowling-green condition, weeded, fed and sprinkled like no others in London. To the passer-by in the 1960s and 1970s the house presented an almost mirage appearance, so cool and fresh and calm amidst the bustle and taxi fumes of Curzon Street.

Behind its serene, dignified façade, however, the Thomas Tilling Group was getting into difficulties; like so much of British commercial life it had become over-extended, complacent, laxly-managed and uncompetitive. Indeed in many ways it was an epitome of the British economy : a large successful firm built up by two generations of energetic Victorian entrepreneurs, enjoying a prosperous middle-age and then falling into comparative decline. It was badly shaken by the recession of the late 1970s and, after three years manoeuvring, was successfully taken over in 1983 by B.T.R. (British Tiles and Rubber, a large conglomerate holding-company with many subsidiaries). B.T.R. immediately started a restructuring exercise. The constructional part of the company, Tilcon, has survived and is still in business, its headquarters now being situated at Knaresborough in Yorkshire. Crewe House itself was once again put on the market and sold in 1984, this time for the substantial sum of thirty-seven million pounds.

Chapter Five

The Royal Embassy of the Kingdom of Saudi Arabia

It was a chance remark at a dinner party that led to a complete change in fortunes for Crewe House. Lady Jacqueline Thomson and her husband Sir Mark were dining with the Saudi Arabian Cultural Attaché at the Gavroche. He happened to say that he was having difficulty finding a suitable building for their embassy. Lady Jacqueline asked if he had looked at Crewe House. It was a building she admired, her grandfather, Lord Reading, having lived opposite it, and she had noticed a FOR SALE notice outside the house.

When the Attaché offered to drive the Thomsons home at the end of dinner, Lady Jacqueline suggested that they go out of their way, through Curzon Street. So it was that Crewe House came to be chosen.

The whole site was bought for £37 million.

Under the ownership of Thomas Tilling the Crewe House site had been enlarged by the purchase of additional property, Charles House in Charles Street and Tilling House in Queen Street, so that when purchased by the Saudi Government in 1984 it covered most of the block between Curzon Street and Charles Street. The old house, facing Curzon Street, was only one part of a larger complex of modern office buildings. Thus it was ideally suited to serve as an embassy; it provided ample accommodation for formal entertaining, staff flats and offices, as well as for a chancery with its own public access separate from the main, formal parts of the building. However, to achieve all this would require substantial reconstruction and remodelling.

Michael Lyell Associates, with John Knight as principal architect, were appointed to redesign and adapt the buildings in 1985, and Tarmac Construction, which was already involved in building the King Fahad Academy in Ealing for the Saudi Government, was awarded the principal building contract. Old Crewe House had been listed Grade II* as being of special architectural or historic interest in 1958, so that listed building consent was necessary before any alterations could be made. An application was submitted in December 1986 but negotiations with Westminster City Council and English Heritage proved complex and consent for the works was not granted till a year later in December 1987, construction beginning in 1988 and being completed in 1990.

The proposals involved the restoration of Old Crewe House, the remodelling of New Crewe House (the large office block added at the back by Thomas Tilling) and Charles House, and the complete demolition and rebuilding of Tilling House in Queen Street.

John Knight, the architect for the work, told the *Financial Times* in November 1987:

> The famous front of Crewe House with its bow windows and lawns will be restored, the porters' lodges and horseshoe carriage drive will be reinstated, and the existing boxy porch will be replaced with a Doric colonnaded portico.
>
> And we have a brief to reinstate the interior – which has been much despoiled over the years – to an appropriate plain English 18th century style with timber panelled rooms, a new staircase, and restored black and white marble floors.

(Fig. 27) The Reception Hall, displaying the needlework frieze of Kaaba cloth, from the Kaaba Kiswah of the Holy Mosque at Mecca.

The reconstruction required considerable ingenuity to incorporate the sophisticated modern services required, and the strict security requirements which formed part of the original architectural brief drawn up by the Saudi Ministry of Foreign Affairs in May 1985. Even before negotiations began with the planners and historic buildings authorities considerable amendments had to be made in the course of preparing the designs, in order to reconcile all the conflicting requirements of the brief which were summarised by the architects under five headings:

To remodel the existing old buildings to achieve the maximum usable floor space.

To devise a plan that would attain a workable relationship between all the functions of an Embassy.

To integrate sophisticated services within buildings which were never designed to accommodate such things.

To conform to all current planning, building and statutory regulations.

To achieve all these objectives while preserving those parts of the new embassy that are listed as being of historic and architectural interest without compromising in any measure well integrated security principles.

The aim was to redesign the three existing interconnecting buildings between Curzon Street and Charles Street to accommodate the offices and reception rooms of the Chancery and Consulate, and to incorporate an underground car park for thirteen cars. The separate building in Queen Street was rebuilt to provide the residential accommodation required by the Westminster Planning Officers. Security considerations made necessary the provision of separate entrances for the public, tradesmen, and diplomatic staff, which added to the complexity of the circulation plans. The main entrance in Curzon Street was to be reserved for the Ambassador, visiting VIPs and the senior staff of the Chancery. All other embassy personnel were to enter from a new consular entrance in Charles Street. Catering and maintenance staff were to have their own entrance in Queen Street, where a vehicular access road was contrived under the rebuilt Tilling House. The public were also to be provided with their own entrance, via the Visa Hall in Charles Street.

All this was achieved with the most scrupulous and respectful care – in particular, the preservation of the character of the façade to Curzon Street. There the only significant alterations were the replacement of Lord Crewe's enclosed porch with an open Tuscan *porte cochère*, and the re-arrangement of the entrance drive. (Fig. 28) Thomas Tilling's central entrance and plain railings were replaced with a horseshoe drive, based on the eighteenth century arrangement shown on Horwood's map of London, and more elaborate wrought iron gates and railings. For security reasons a pair of little octagonal porters' lodges were built flanking the

(Fig. 28) The exterior of the Royal Embassy of Saudi Arabia. The pediment carries the emblem of a date palm over crossed swords, symbolising that prosperity can only be had through justice.

new gates to Curzon Street. These were treated as simple stuccoed classical structures to match the façade of Crewe House, their elevations being based on designs supplied by John Martin Robinson (then of the London Division of English Heritage). The bland 1960s façade of Charles House was also faced in stucco and given classical mouldings and small paned sash windows to make a match with the fine Georgian houses in the rest of Charles Street.

Not much of the original eighteenth century work (apart from some mouldings and window shutters) survived inside old Crewe House, and nothing of the Wharncliffe period. Even Lord Crewe's Edwardian work had been much modified under Thomas Tilling's ownership. His double-height entrance hall with its coved plaster ceiling and black and white marble floor survived, however, as did a pair of splendid Georgian chimney-pieces introduced by him, a marble one from the North Room, which has been re-used in the Ambassador's room, and an interesting carved wooden rococo design in the east wing, retained *in situ*.

The original cantilevered stone stairs with a wrought iron balustrade had been removed by Thomas Tilling. They have been replaced with a more spaciously designed staircase of carved mahogany with turned balusters. Matching mahogany joinery has been installed in some of the other principal rooms facing Curzon Street. Surviving elements of the original structure, such as the sash windows, have been carefully repaired, Haymills joinery undertaking the woodwork contract. Some of the old fabric proved to be rather insubstantial by modern standards including the central pediment which is made of lath and plaster on timber studwork rather than brickwork. But it was kept nevertheless for historical reasons. The roof was also reslated using grey Port Madoc slates from Wales to match the old ones.

The later buildings at the back of the site were not covered by the

(Fig. 29) The Royal Embassy of Saudi Arabia. The lettering on the flag reads: "There is no God but God, Muhammad is the Prophet of God".

(Fig. 30) The interior of the Embassy's reception room.

(Fig. 31) The Reception Hall, where a weekly majlis is held.

(Figs. 32 & 33) The leather wall hangings bought for the Dining Room by the 1st Earl of Wharncliffe, circa 1876, on the advice of Sir Ambrose Poynter RA.

listing, so there the architects had a freer hand. New Crewe House, the 1960s block by Gunton & Gunton, was gutted to create a large new reception hall. This has been treated in an authentically Arabian manner with marble work, Islamic tiles, and decorative plaster work including arches and friezes the details of which are based on traditional models in the Middle East. This large and elaborate room comes as an unexpected surprise after the understated stucco architecture of the Curzon Street facade, but it makes an unusual late twentieth century architectural contribution to the long evolution of Crewe House.

The Reception Hall was designed by Michael Lyell & Associates drawing inspiration from traditional Islamic buildings in the Middle East. It was devised to display the needlework frieze of Kaaba cloth, from the Kaaba Kiswah of the Holy Mosque at Mecca. Beautifully embroidered with Koranic inscriptions in gold and silver on black velvet, this was a special gift from the King of Saudi Arabia to the Embassy and was adapted for display in its present position by the Royal School of Needlework.

The elaborate fibrous plasterwork executed between November 1990 and July 1991 was carried out by Troika Architectural Mouldings Ltd. of Sheffield, to detail designs by Michael Lyell & Associates, cost £150,000, and won the 1992 Plasterers' Trophy for decorative plastering. It comprises the pendentive *muquarnas* cornice (beneath the Kaaba cloth), panels of carved stylised foliage cusped Islamic arches and star pattern. The climax of the room is the *muquarnas* niche twenty feet high and twelve feet wide. *Muquarnas* (pendentive overhanging prismatic sections) are a traditional Islamic decoration usually executed in stone and wood and are built up in situ from hundreds of prismatic sections. To achieve this effect in plaster is something of a *tour de force* and required a special effort on the part of the plasterers. A 1:5 scale model was made before work began. The body of the niche was then constructed of four equal sections cast in glass reinforced gypsum in the Sheffield works, using extra-strong British Gypsum Crystacal R plaster. The extended pendants were then added by hand on site and comprise some two hundred and thirty-two pieces in six different forms. The whole of the plasterwork has been painted stark white and is lit by low voltage spot lights which enhance its dramatic impact. (Fig. 31)

The rest of the Reception Hall is faced in marble and tiles of traditional Islamic patterns. The tiles were imported. The geometrical floor of Thosos Marble was designed by the architects and is inlaid with yellow and green Spanish and Italian marble, while the columns are clad in pure white Thosos marble, enlivened by cast plaster decoration also by Troikas. Another traditional Islamic architectural feature of the new Reception Hall are the *mashrabiya* screens of lattice pattern mahogany made by Senior Carmichael, the special joinery contractors. These are used to close off the Diwan, the private reception area used by the ambassador and his principal guests, from the main ceremonial part of the Reception Hall.

The life of the house has now taken on a completely different character, far removed from the somewhat dreary nature of the office routine of the years since it ceased to be a family home. It is perhaps not too fanciful to think that its new persona has what one might call the spirit of an extended family – that of the people of Saudi Arabia.

Nobody knows quite how many Saudi Arabians there are in Britain, as it is very much a floating population. There are few permanent residents. However several thousand Saudis own houses or flats in Britain, mostly in London, and come for frequent visits especially in the summer, and every year many others rent places. Apart from them there are, at any one time, about one thousand students scattered around the country engaged in full-time higher education.

To all these people the Embassy offers a feeling of home. On every Wednesday evening between 6 and 8 p.m. (except in Ramadan when it is 10 to 12 p.m.) the Ambassador holds a *majlis* or assembly in the splendid marble hall with its familiar architecture and its decorations, based on the inscriptions in the Holy Mosque at Mecca. The holding of a regular *majlis* is very ancient Arabian tradition. The King in Saudi Arabia and all his provincial governors hold them each week, to which anyone may come to present a petition or make a complaint.

The Ambassador is most punctilious about his *majlis*, never accepting any invitation that would conflict with it, nor cancelling it if he is feeling unwell. It is mainly intended for Saudis who are visiting London, though anyone (male) is welcome.

Religion naturally plays an important part in the everyday life of the Embassy. Five times a day the call to prayer is broadcast to every room, sometimes made live by one of the Embassy staff who, as it happens, is a Egyptian, and sometimes with a recording of one of the outstanding *muezzins* of Mecca.

Although the security arrangements have to be stringent and possibly startling to naive visitors, there is an agreeably informal atmosphere, with people stopping for little chats and a friendly cup of tea, which those who work there say they appreciate.

After so long and varied a history, Crewe House has become one of the most spacious and impressive embassy buildings in London – a proud presence in Mayfair for one of Britain's principal Middle East allies.

Appendix

Contractors and Craftsmen Employed in the Royal Embassy of the Kingdom of Saudi Arabia, Curzon Street, London W.1.

Architects & Interior Designers	Michael Lyell Associates Mr John Knight
Project Managers	Symonds Tramor Mr Peter McCartney
Construction Cost Consultants	Symonds Mr Alan Brenton
Main Contractor	Tarmac Construction Ltd.
Fitting out Contractor	Interiors International Mr Brian Metheringham
Marblework	Shellreach Mr Gerald Cruickshank
Special Joinery	Senior Carmichael/W. J. White & Co. Mr Rupert Senior/Mr P. White
Plasterwork	Troika Mr T. Wright
Framing and Gilding	J. Campbell Ltd./Gerval Associates Mr R. Hogben/Ms M. P. Gerval
Architectural Metalwork	J. Desmond Ltd. Mr J. Desmond
Ceramic Tiling	The Tiling Company
Hand Tufted Carpets	Vsoske Joyce Ireland
Architectural Ironmongery	Elementer Industrial Design Ltd. Mr Peter Thorley
Chandeliers	Arnold Montrose
Kaaba Cloth (Tapestry)	Royal School of Needlework/ SAM Design

Index